Nature Made

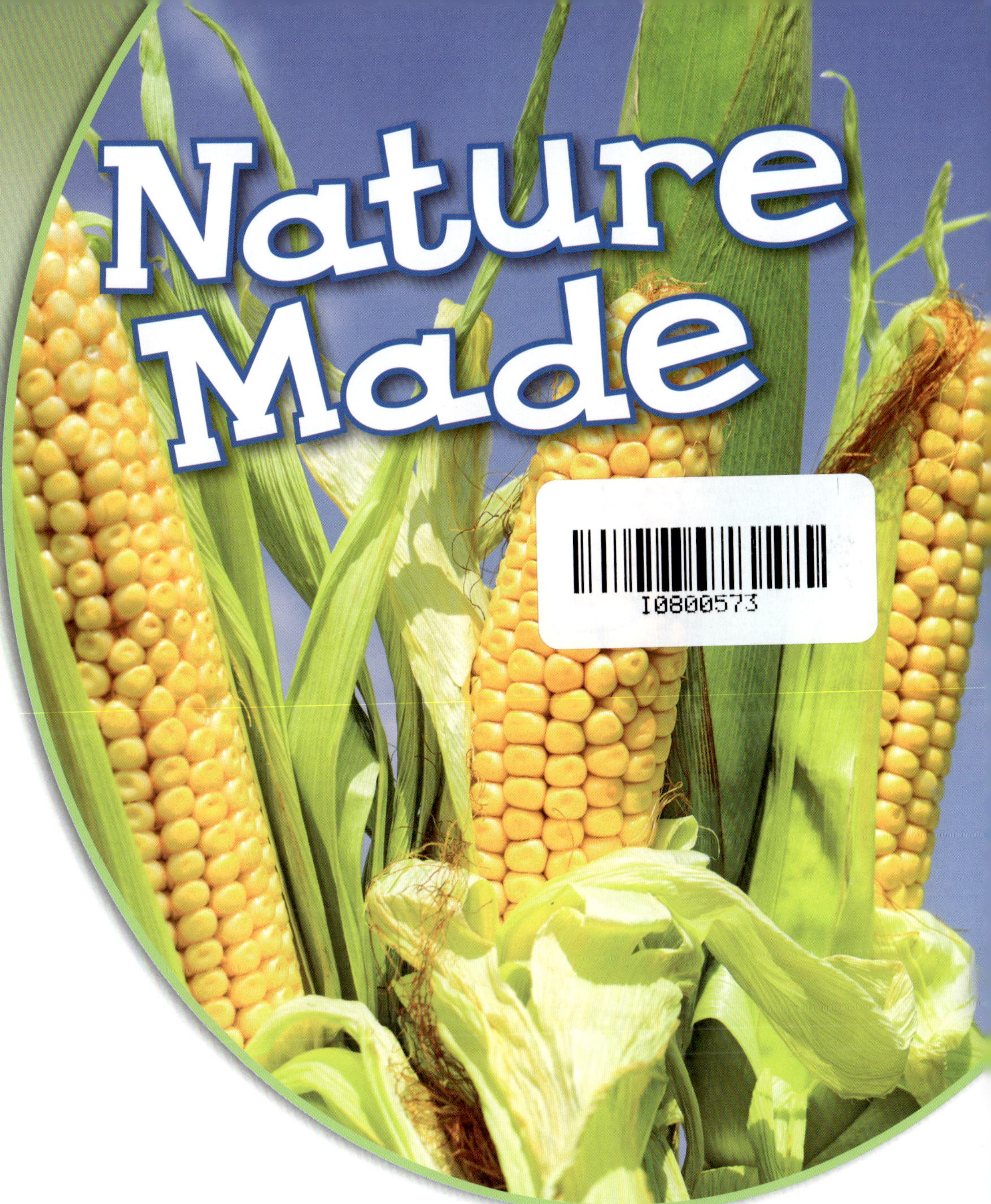

Anne Montgomery

People need things to live.

Earth gives us many things.

We use some to make things we need.

Trees grow.

We use trees
for wood.

The sun shines.

We use the sun for **energy**.

Rocks cover the land.

We use rocks to build.

Sand covers beaches.

We use sand to
make bricks.

Metal is in rocks.

We use metal to make tools.

Plants grow.

We eat what **nature** gives us.

Let's Do Science!

What can you build from nature? Try this!

What to Get

- ❑ glue or string
- ❑ rocks, twigs, leaves, and other things from nature
- ❑ scissors

What to Do

1. Use your materials to make a tiny house. Make a floor, roof, and walls. Attach them with glue or string.

2. How is your tiny house the same as a real house? How is it different? Are any of the materials the same?

Glossary

Earth—the planet we live on

energy—power

nature—things in the world not made by people

Index

Your Turn!

Look at the picture above or look outside. What things come from nature? What things did people make?

Consultants

Sally Creel, Ed.D.
Curriculum Consultant

Leann Iacuone, M.A.T., NBCT, ATC
Riverside Unified School District

Jill Tobin
California Teacher of the Year
Semi-Finalist
Burbank Unified School District

Publishing Credits

Conni Medina, M.A.Ed., *Managing Editor*
Lee Aucoin, *Creative Director*
Diana Kenney, M.A.Ed., NBCT, *Senior Editor*
Lynette Tanner, *Editor*
Lexa Hoang, *Designer*
Hillary Dunlap, *Photo Editor*
Rachelle Cracchiolo, M.S.Ed., *Publisher*

Image Credits: p.13 brianindia /Alamy; p.17 Don Mason/Blend Images/Alamy; p.4 James Stockwin/Alamy; p.11 iStock; pp.18–19 (illustrations) Rusty Kinnunen; all other images from Shutterstock.

Library of Congress Cataloging-in-Publication Data

Montgomery, Anne (Anne Diana), author.
Nature made / Anne Montgomery.
pages cm
Summary: "It is time to learn about things we use from nature."—Provided by publisher.
Audience: K to grade 3.
Includes index.
ISBN 978-1-4807-4528-5 (pbk.) —
ISBN 978-1-4807-5137-8 (ebook)
1. Nature—Juvenile literature. 2. Natural resources—Juvenile literature. 3. Readers (Primary) I. Title.
QH48.M617 2015
508—dc23
2014008927

Teacher Created Materials
5301 Oceanus Drive
Huntington Beach, CA 92649-1030
http://www.tcmpub.com

ISBN 978-1-4807-4528-5

Printed by: 51497
Printed in: Taiwan